YEAR 2

COMPREHENSION AND VOCABULARY

Do you need to go back to the basics and practise comprehension and your vocabulary? Let's read together and learn ...

Parents and carers are encouraged to read the explanation and practice sections with their children.

Victoria Hazell

Illustrated by
Janice Bowles

Back to Basics Comprehension and Vocabulary Year 2

Reprinted 2015, 2016, 2018, 2022

ISBN: 978 1 74215 916 4

Published by Pascal Press
PO Box 250
Glebe NSW 2037
www.pascalpress.com.au
contact@pascalpress.com.au

Author: Victoria Hazell
Publisher: Lynn Dickinson
Editors: Shelley Barons and Kerry Davies AE
Design and illustration: Janice Bowles
Cover design: Deb Snibson, MAPG
Printed by Wai Man Book Binding (China) Ltd.

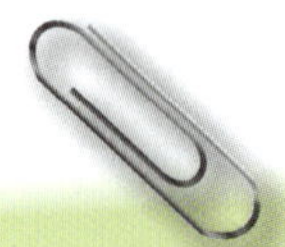

Acknowledgements
The author is grateful to Blake Education for kindly granting permission to reproduce extracts and illustrations from the following books:

Page 10, Lisa Thompson, *The Great Balancing Act*, illustrated by Andy & Inga Hamilton, Storylands, 2009.

Page 12, Wendy Blaxland, *Crazy Chewing Gum*, illustrated by Jan D'Silva, Gigglers, 2005.

Page 16, Lisa Thompson, *The Gwibber*, illustrated by Luke Jurevicius, Arthur Moody & Toby Quarmby, Storylands, 2009.

Page 18, Lisa Thompson, *The Big Kidnap*, illustrated by Ritva Voutila, Storylands, 2008.

Page 22, Lisa Thompson, *Pirate School*, illustrated by Craig Smith & Lew Keilar, Storylands, 2007.

Page 26, Ian Rohr & Laura Sieveking, *Transport*, Go Facts, 2009.

Page 30, Paul McEvoy, *Reptiles*, Go Facts, 2002.

Page 32, Ian Rohr, *Extreme Mammals*, Go Facts, 2008.

Page 36, Ian Rohr, *Mountains*, Go Facts, 2007.

Page 38, Mark Stafford, *Architecture*, Go Facts, 2008.

Contents & Checklist

ABOUT THIS BOOK

This book is designed to review essential Comprehension and Vocabulary skills required in Year 2. It provides detailed explanations of how to comprehend fiction and non-fiction texts in a literal, interpretive and applied manner. Each comprehension unit features a text extract with questions requiring literal, interpretive and applied comprehension of the text.

Literal comprehension:
What did the author tell you? Refer directly to the text to find the answers.

Interpretive comprehension:
What did the author intend you to understand? Read back over the text and think about what you can conclude from the facts you are given.

Applied comprehension:
*What do **you** think?* Relate what you have read to real-life situations and your existing knowledge of the world.

Parents or carers are encouraged to read the full explanations, on pages 8–9 for fiction and pages 24–25 for non-fiction, with their children before they do the practice units, and to discuss the glossary words under each text extract.

If further instruction is required, provide this book to the class teacher for review. A plan can then be devised between parent or carer and the school to ensure that all basic concepts are fully understood and consolidated.

Helpful features

★ **10 Top tips** are provided in full on pages 6 and 7 and are featured on the Practise pages. Read the tips carefully before reading them with your child, explaining any difficult words to ensure that each concept is fully understood.

★ **5 Vocabulary units** (Units 3, 7, 11, 15 and 19) feature activities using the 100 high-frequency words relevant to Year 2 students.

★ **5 Quick quizzes** (Units 4, 8, 12, 16 and 20) feature words used in the preceding stories and reinforce understanding of specific vocabulary found in the texts.

★ **100 High-frequency words** are provided in the centre of the book to be removed, laminated and cut out to make game cards for extra practice (see page 5).

★ **3 Tests** on pages 42–44, two comprehension tests and a high-frequency words test, are to be done on completion of all 20 units. These tests will check that the skills have been consolidated.

★ **BOB time! Back Of the Book.** At the end of most exercises, BOB will remind children to check the Answer section on pages 45–47 to make sure they are on the right track.

Ideas for using the Game Cards

The game cards in the centre of the book feature 100 high-frequency words that Year 2 children should be able to recognise, read and spell.

Two players

Player 1 flashes a card and Player 2 reads each word and spells it out accurately (without looking at the card).

Player 1 looks at a card and reads each word aloud (one at a time). Player 2 repeats the word and then writes it down. If a word is incorrectly spelled, take time to practise and then ask to be tested once more.

One player

1. Place all the same colour cards face down in a pile. Turn them over one at a time and read the words on the card.
2. Put the card face down on a second pile and quickly write down the words before you forget them.
3. Check that you have spelled them correctly and move on to the next card.
4. Score yourself and try to improve each time. Practise the misspelled words by writing them each five times.

Place all cards face up.
Sort into two piles:
Pile 1: Words I know
Pile 2: Words I am learning
Read aloud each word in Pile 2 and add it to Pile 1 when you know all the words on the card.

Australian Curriculum Year 2

Listen for specific purposes and information, including instructions, and extend students' own and others' ideas in discussions (ACELY1666)
Read less predictable texts with phrasing and fluency by combining contextual, semantic, grammatical and phonic knowledge using text processing strategies, for example monitoring meaning, predicting, rereading and self-correcting (ACELY1669)
Use comprehension strategies to build literal and inferred meaning and begin to analyse texts by drawing on growing knowledge of context, language and visual features and print and multimodal text structures (ACELY1670)

10 TOP TIPS

Helpful tips to gain full comprehension of a text

1

Main Idea

When we read, we can use features in the text to determine the main idea of the text. Looking for headings, bold print, pictures, captions and diagrams can help us work out what the text is mostly about.

So, look at the text and then ask:

"What is the main idea?"

2

Predictions

When we read, we think about what might happen next and make predictions based on what we know and what we have read so that we can find out the sequence of events.

So, read the text and then ask:

"What happens next?"

3

Cause and Effect

When we read, we can think about what caused something to happen and what the effect was. If you read a story or a newspaper article, it will always tell you what has happened and what caused it to happen.

So, read the text and then ask:

"What happened?" and "What caused it to happen?"

4

Connections

When we read, we make connections between what we know, other things we have read and the text we are reading.

So, read the text and then ask:

"Does this remind me of something?"

"Is this situation like something that has happened to me?"

5

Inferences

When we read, we form our own ideas, or make inferences, about what we are reading. We can use clues in the text to figure out what else the author wants us to know.

So, read the text and then ask:

"What did the author want me to believe?"

"What was I supposed to find out?"

6

Monitoring

When we read, we should monitor our reading to make sure we understand what the author is saying, and have strategies to "fix" any comprehension problems as they arise. So, as you read the text, ask:

"Is this making sense?"
"Do I need to re-read?"
"Are there any text clues to help me fill in the missing information?"

7

Text Purpose

When we read, we should ask ourselves what the purpose of the text is. Did the author write to entertain the readers, to inform us about a particular topic, or to persuade the readers to think a certain way?
Read the text and then ask:
"What was the author's intention?"

8

Fact or Opinion?

When we read, we make judgements about what we are reading. We decide whether it is a fact or just an opinion and we should give reasons for our decision.
So, read the text and then ask:

"Is this a fact that can be proven?"
"Is this an opinion, someone's view?"

9

Visualising

When we read, we visualise what is happening while we read the text. Creating a movie in our minds helps us understand the setting, the characters and the events of the story.
So, read the text and then ask:
"Can I picture this new information?"
"What can I see, hear, smell or feel?"

10

Summarising

When we read, we summarise the information we are given.
To summarise, we identify the most important ideas in the text and explain them in our own words. So, read the text and then ask:

"What were the most important ideas?"

FICTION

Here is a poem from me to you
A poem that will help you read, it's true
Words are not hard when in a long line
The trick is to get help time after time

Reading is like sport; you must train every day
A coach can help you when you need it, okay?
Some of the words can be hard or new
A coach can give you a very big clue

Remember that reading is fun to do
Stories and facts to entertain you!

Remember: A reading coach could be a teacher, parent or other adult who can help you.

LITERAL COMPREHENSION

LITERAL COMPREHENSION

We understand what the text says. Understanding exactly what we have read is important so that we can then answer some questions about the text.

We can go back at any time to check what we understand.

We practise

What is the poem about?	Reading
What is the message?	Practise
Who can help?	A coach, a parent or a teacher
What do you need to remember?	It's fun to do

Now that we understand what has been read, let's write a response in a full sentence using the questions ...

What is the poem about?	The poem is about learning to read.
What is the message?	The message is that I need to practise every day.
Who can help?	A coach, a parent or a teacher can help me read.
What do you need to remember?	Reading is a fun thing to do, and stories and facts can entertain me.

Do you agree with the answers? Check the text to make sure.

INTERPRETIVE COMPREHENSION

INTERPRETIVE COMPREHENSION

We understand what the text says and then link information or ideas together to get a greater meaning. We can then answer some more questions about the text.

In the poem, what does the author want people to do?

We practise

Practise reading every day.

We can interpret this because the text tells us *Reading is like sport; you must train every day*. The author thinks people should practise reading every day.

Why should you do what the author suggests?

I will get better at reading, and I will enjoy stories and finding out facts.

The text tells us *Some of the words can be hard or new / A coach can give you a very big clue*. We can interpret this to mean that others can help when we read. A "reading coach" could be a teacher, a parent or older sibling, a tutor or other helper. *Remember that reading is fun to do / Stories and facts to entertain you!* This tells us that we will enjoy hearing stories and finding out facts.

Do you agree with the interpretations and the answers?

Check the text to make sure.

We can go back at any time to confirm what we understand.

APPLIED COMPREHENSION

APPLIED COMPREHENSION

We understand the text, then add what we have learned to what we already know and draw conclusions. We will be able to answer questions that go **beyond** the text.

We practise

Read the poem again. Why should you get help and practise reading?

I should get help to make reading easier and I should practise so I improve.

The text tells us *Reading is like sport; you must train every day / A coach can help you when you need it, okay?* This reminds us that, if we practise reading every day and ask for help with hard words when we need it, our reading will improve and will soon become fun.

How will improving your reading help you?

I will recognise more words and be able to read sentences better on my own. I can enjoy stories and will improve my general knowledge about topics I do not know about.

The text tells us *Words are not hard when in a long line / The trick is to get help time after time*. This reminds us that with help we can do it. The text says reading gives *Stories and facts to entertain you!* This reminds us that reading can be enjoyable as well as teaching us new information.

Can you use what you already know to provide your own answers?

THE GREAT BALANCING ACT

Read this with a grown-up and discuss any tricky words.

FICTION

Wonderful Wilma was upset. Her monkeys, Momo and Bobo, had climbed the highest flagpole and could not get down. "If only the Zoomelli Family were here," she cried. "Where are the acrobats when I need them?"

"Never fear," said Ringmaster Roy. "I shall get the circus bus and climb on top of it with my ladder to get the monkeys." But the ladder snapped and the Ringmaster tumbled to the ground.

Amazing Anton had an idea.
"Edna the elephant and I will climb on top of the bus, and I shall reach the monkeys with my rope."
Edna the Elephant climbed on the bus. Amazing Anton held on tight. Edna's legs shook. But Amazing Anton threw the rope so hard that he went with it!

The wind blew, and the flagpole swayed. "This is terrible," cried Wilma. "Who will save Momo and Bobo?"

"Never fear," said the Ringmaster. "Max Manyhands has an idea."

Max Manyhands strapped his juggling chairs to his back. He climbed the bus. He stacked his juggling chairs on top of Edna and reached for the monkeys with a hoop. But the monkeys would not let go.

A fly buzzed past Edna's eyes.
She swooshed it with her trunk. But as she moved, the chairs moved. Bendy Betty quickly climbed up and grabbed the chairs.

The Zoomelli Family appeared just in time! They calmly climbed the bus and Edna, the chairs and Bendy Betty, and then on to each other. Grandpa Zoomelli walked along a rope to Momo and Bobo. The monkeys climbed happily into his arms.

Now everyone had to get down!

***by Lisa Thompson** (abridged)*

GLOSSARY

We practise

acrobats	people who perform tumbling acts in the circus
juggling	keeping objects in the air by tossing and catching
calmly	peacefully – slowly and carefully

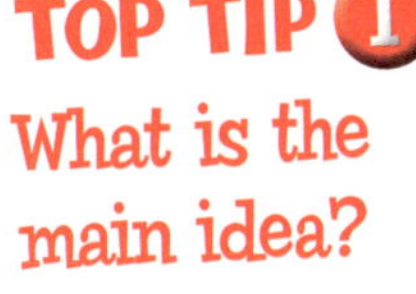

 Who did the monkeys, Momo and Bobo, belong to?

The monkeys belonged to ___

 What sort of circus animal was Edna?

___

 What made the flagpole sway?

___

 What did Max Manyhands use to try to reach the monkeys?

___

 Why wouldn't the monkeys let go of the flagpole for Max?

___

 Why did Edna swoosh the fly with her trunk?

___

 Why do you think she is called Bendy Betty?

___

 Why did the monkeys happily go to Grandpa Zoomelli?

___

 Were Momo and Bobo in danger?

___

 Did all the circus people risk their lives to save the monkeys?

___

BOB time!

UNIT 2

CRAZY CHEWING GUM

Read this with a grown-up and discuss any tricky words.

FICTION

Mum hates chewing gum. She won't have it in the house. "Nasty stuff," she says. "It gets EVERYWHERE!"

So I want to make my own. I look on the internet for recipes. Super Strawberry sounds good. I shut my door and mix. I'm just adding the fluoro pink food colouring when Mum knocks on the door. "Declan, what's that smell? Are you experimenting again?"

"Don't come in," I call, sweeping it all into my drawer. "It's a surprise." Blackie pushes the door open. She shoves her nose in the drawer. One of the glue powders tips into my mixture. "Out of there!" I yell. I pull Blackie's head out. The gum is stuck to her nose. Her nose is bright fluoro pink! Mum goes ballistic. "Declan!" she shouts. Blackie tries to wipe the chewing gum off. Now Blackie has pink stuff on her paw.

Dad comes home and Blackie runs and jumps on him. Bright pink strings hang from his jacket. "Hey, this is my good suit," says Dad, wiping it off. The pink strings stick to his hands.
"For goodness sakes, Declan," he says.

"Nobody move," Mum orders.
"Now Declan, what is this gum-glue?"

"Chewing gum, Mum," I admit. I pull out a lump and pop it in my mouth. Big mistake! My teeth are stuck together.

"Right," says Dad. "We need to get some help."

They take Blackie to the vet first. "Her fur will grow back soon," the vet says. "As for her pink nose, maybe it will wear off. I've never seen anything like it." Next we go to the dentist. His drill overheats. He adds the cost of the drill to our bill.

It'll take me months to pay everyone back. Mum says I will have to live with my pink spotted carpet. Unless I invent something to clean it off! Let's just switch on the computer ...

by Wendy Blaxland *(abridged)*

GLOSSARY

recipe	a list of instructions to make something to eat
fluoro pink	very bright pink
ballistic	crazily angry, very cross
bill	the amount of money to be paid

You practise

TOP TIP 2
Predict what happens next.

1. Where did Declan find the recipe?

Declan found the recipe ______________________________

2. What did Blackie the dog do to make Declan yell at her?

____

3. What happened to Blackie's nose?

____

4. What happened to Declan's father's suit?

____

5. Why was Declan's mother cross?

____

6. Why was Declan's father cross?

____

7. Why was the dentist cross?

____

8. Why was the chewing gum even stickier than usual?

____

9. Was the mess all Blackie's fault?

____

10. What will happen if Declan makes carpet cleaner?

____

BOB time!

VOCABULARY 1

HIGH-FREQUENCY WORDS 1–20

The words featured in this unit are on the red word cards.

1 Words and meaning

For each word below, look at the shape, the sound blend and spelling. Write a sentence using the word to make sure you know its meaning.

the ______________________________

he ______________________________

be ______________________________

but ______________________________

which ______________________________

out ______________________________

into ______________________________

no ______________________________

made ______________________________

long ______________________________

2 Pattern practice

Write each word twice to help you see the letter patterns.

of	________	________	them	________	________
for	________	________	has	________	________
this	________	________	make	________	________
what	________	________	over	________	________
their	________	________	little	________	________

BOB time!

You practise

QUICK QUIZ 1

Unit 1 **The Great Balancing Act** Unit 2 **Crazy Chewing Gum**

1 Writing sentences

Write each word from the word bank in a sentence.

wonderful	upset	monkeys	climbed	highest
fear	climb	elephant	juggling	happily

a I had a wonderful birthday party with my friends.

b ______

c ______

d ______

e ______

f ______

g ______

h ______

i ______

j ______

Jumbled words

Unjumble and write these mixed-up words from the word bank.

chewing	gum	smell	nose	jumps
pink	glue	dentist	drill	computer

a hcwengi ______

b umg ______

c lelms ______

d lrild ______

e sjmup ______

f kinp ______

g elug ______

h seno ______

i stendit ______

j pmocture ______

BOB time!

THE GWIBBER

Read this with a grown-up and discuss any tricky words.

FICTION

Gog was excited. "Come quickly," he yelled to Binks, the elf. "I want to show you something special." Binks ran outside. "I found a Gwibber in the forest," said Gog. He pointed to a giant winged beast on the roof. "Muddy pups!" said Binks. "Look at the size of it! It will eat us out of house and home."

"Gwibbers make great guard dogs," said Gog.

"You are a giant. You don't need a guard dog," said Binks.

The Gwibber flew off the roof. He was hungry. He wanted something to eat. The Gwibber ate all the beans in the vegetable patch. "Muddy pups!" said Binks. "All our beans are gone." The Gwibber looked around the garden. Now he was thirsty and he wanted something to drink. The Gwibber drank all the water out of the fish pond. "Muddy pups!" said Binks. "All our water is gone."

The Gwibber walked to the fence. He was tired. He wanted somewhere to sleep. The Gwibber dug a hole in the garden. "Muddy pups!" said Binks. "Our garden is gone." When the Gwibber woke up, he was lonely. He wanted to go into the house. So he scratched at the front door. "Muddy pups!" said Binks. "Our front door is gone."

That night the Gwibber could not sleep. He screeched and howled all night long. "Muddy pups!" said Binks. "I need my sleep! I have to do something about that Gwibber!" Binks stormed off into the forest. She scratched and screeched. She squeaked and squawked. Binks made every Gwibber noise she knew. Gog's Gwibber heard the noises. He flew off to find the other Gwibbers.

"That's wonderful! Happy muddy pups!" said Binks. "The Gwibber is gone!"

by Lisa Thompson *(abridged)*

GLOSSARY

forest	area covered in tall trees
winged beast	animal with wings
guard dog	dog that protects
lonely	alone and wanting a friend

You practise

TOP TIP 3
Think about cause and effect.
What happened?
What caused it?

1 Why was Gog excited?

Gog was excited because ____________________

2 Why was Binks worried when she saw the size of the Gwibber?

____

3 Why didn't Binks think Gog needed a guard dog?

____

4 What did the Gwibber eat when he flew off the roof?

____

5 Why was the water in the fish pond important to Binks?

____

6 Why was Binks upset about where the Gwibber slept?

____

7 Why did the Gwibber want to go inside when he felt lonely?

____

8 Do you think that Gog would really miss the Gwibber?

____

9 Why did Binks keep saying, "Muddy pups"?

____

10 Why would Binks have slept well after the Gwibber was gone?

____

BOB time!

THE BIG KIDNAP

Read this with a grown-up and discuss any tricky words.

FICTION

Pebble would not go to bed. She was too busy being wild. She yelled as she swung through the jungle. River tried to get her to go to bed. Pebble would not listen. She just got wilder. Luna tried to get her to go bed. Pebble would not listen. She laughed wildly and got louder. Rex tried to get Pebble to go to bed – or else! Pebble ran deep into the jungle.

Everyone could hear her but nobody could find her. Nobody was getting any sleep. Everyone was tired and grumpy. Something had to be done. Together they came up with a plan.

That night, River and Brock set a trap. They caught Pebble in a big net. Pebble screeched, "Let me go! Let me go!" But she could not escape. Pebble screeched and wriggled. "Let me go! Let me go!" The dinosaurs carried her to the top of a hill. Tickles picked up the net. She flew with Pebble over the mountain. Pebble screeched, wriggled and squawked. "Let me go! Let me go!"

Tickles took Pebble to the other side of the island. Tickles left her on a soft bed of feathers. Luna sat in a tree singing sleepy songs. Leo made Pebble some hot milk. Soon Pebble was fast asleep. Then one by one, they all fell fast asleep. The island was quiet.

That night, everyone had lots of wonderful dreams. Even Pebble!

by Lisa Thompson *(abridged)*

GLOSSARY

jungle	wild tropical rainforest
grumpy	bad mood
trap	a tool to catch something

You practise

TOP TIP 4
Make connections between what you read and what you know.

1. Why wouldn't Pebble go to bed?

Pebble wouldn't go to bed because ______________________

2. What happened when Luna tried to get Pebble to go to bed?

____

3. What was the plan to get Pebble to go to sleep?

____

4. What happened when they trapped Pebble?

____

5. Was Pebble happy running wild in the forest? How do you know?

____

6. Did the dinosaurs look after Pebble on the other side of the mountain?

____

7. Why was Luna singing in the tree?

____

8. Why did all the dinosaurs go to sleep when Pebble did?

____

9. Was Pebble naughty?

____

10. Was the plan to make Pebble go to bed too mean?

____

BOB time!

VOCABULARY 2

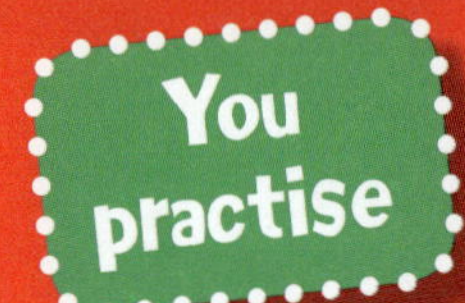

HIGH-FREQUENCY WORDS 21–40

The words featured in this unit are on the blue word cards.

and	said	did	I	her
was	then	very	were	first
from	more	a	if	down
all	than	on	she	after

Opposites

Find words in the word bank that have the opposite meanings to these words (opposites are called antonyms).

a him ______________________

b up ______________________

c none ______________________

d now ______________________

e less ______________________

f before ______________________

g he ______________________

h last ______________________

i to ______________________

j off ______________________

Rainbow words

Choose ten words from the word bank to write, making each letter a different colour.

______________________ ______________________

______________________ ______________________

______________________ ______________________

______________________ ______________________

______________________ ______________________

BOB time!

You practise

QUICK QUIZ 2

Unit 5 The Gwibber Unit 6 The Big Kidnap

1 Word grid

Circle each word from the word bank in the word grid below.

excited	quickly	pups	house	hole
eat	fish	yelled	tired	forest

e	x	c	i	t	e	d	r	s	s	e
h	s	q	u	i	c	k	l	y	h	a
u	w	p	s	r	f	o	r	e	s	t
h	o	u	s	e	s	k	t	l	e	g
t	u	p	n	d	h	h	o	l	e	s
f	i	s	h	g	e	l	r	e	d	i
n	t	a	c	t	i	e	e	d	l	c

2 Fill the gaps

Fill in the blanks below using words from the word bank.

wild	yelled	jungle	louder	sleep
plan	net	island	feathers	songs

Jem and Oscar made a __________ to go on a __________ adventure! They packed enough food for a week in the __________. Then they took a boat out to a far-off __________ and looked for somewhere to __________ that night. As they searched, Jem thought he could hear music. "Can you hear someone singing __________?" he asked. "Yes I can," Oscar replied. "And it seems to be getting __________." Suddenly, a tribal chief appeared, wearing a headdress made from __________ . "WHO ARE YOU?" he __________. Before the boys could answer, the chief threw a __________ over them and tied them up tightly. This was NOT the adventure they'd had in mind!

BOB time!

PIRATE SCHOOL

Read this with a grown-up and discuss any tricky words.

FICTION

When Barnacle Bill came aboard, the crew of *The Black Beast* got a huge surprise. Barnacle Bill was the head of the Pirate School ship and he wasn't happy. "Whirling whales!" said Barnacle Bill.

"What kind of pirates are you? You have forgotten how to be bold, fierce and nasty pirates. It's back to school for the lot of you."

"Pirate School?" said Red Beard and his crew.

"Yes. Now get to your lessons," yelled Barnacle Bill.

First was sword-fighting class. Captain Red Beard cut his finger. He did not like the sight of blood. His legs went wobbly. His crew got wobbly legs too. Barnacle Bill shook his head and raised his sword. "What kind of pirates are you?" he cried.

Then there was a cannon-firing class. The Captain's red beard got burnt when the cannon fired. Black soot covered the crew. "Now you're looking like fierce pirates!" said Colin the cannon master. Barnacle Bill just shook his head. "What kind of pirates are you?" he cried.

Treasure-hunting class was on Friday. The crew were all happy to go to this class. Captain Red Beard was not very good at adding or subtracting. His sharing skills were also very bad. His teacher almost walked the plank!

That night, Captain Red Beard and his crew remembered how to be pirates. They showed Barnacle Bill exactly what kind of pirates they were. Quickly and quietly, they set to work stealing Barnacle Bill's treasure!

"Thanks for the treasure!" shouted Captain Red Beard. "You see, we are bold, fierce and clever pirates!"

The crew all cheered as they sailed away.

by Lisa Thompson *(abridged)*

We practise

GLOSSARY

aboard	on the ship deck	**nasty**	mean
crew	sailors who sail the ship	**exactly**	very clearly, precisely
fierce	angry, frightening		

You practise

TOP TIP 5
Use clues to infer what else the author is saying.

1. Who was Barnacle Bill?

Barnacle Bill was ______________________

2. What did he think the pirates had forgotten?

____

3. How was he going to teach them?

____

4. What classes did the crew of *The Black Beast* attend?

____

5. Was Captain Red Beard good at sword fighting?

____

6. Did Barnacle Bill want them to be better pirates?

____

7. Were the crew of *The Black Beast* very clever?

____

8. Why would the crew have been laughing at Barnacle Bill?

____

9. Did Pirate School make the pirates bold, fierce and nasty?

____

10. Would Barnacle Bill chase Captain Red Beard and the crew?

____

BOB time!

NON-FICTION

Earwigs

Earwigs do not eat ears or live in your ears! They do not crawl into your ear and through to your brain to eat your brain while you are asleep! Earwigs eat plant and animal material. Many earwigs really like pollen and they fly from flower to flower to eat it. Earwigs look harmful because of their pincers but they are harmless to humans.

Many animals eat earwigs – frogs, lizards, spiders, praying mantises, ants and some birds feed on earwigs regularly. They are an important part of the food chain.

LITERAL COMPREHENSION

We understand what the text says. Understanding exactly what we have read is important so that we can then answer some questions about the text.

We can go back at any time to check what we understand.

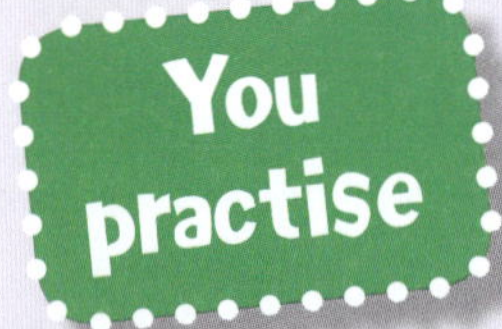

Do earwigs live in your ear?

Earwigs do not live in your ear.

What do earwigs eat?

Earwigs eat plant and animal material and some like pollen.

What likes to eat earwigs?

Frogs, lizards, spiders, praying mantises, ants and some birds like to eat earwigs.

Do you agree with the answers? Check the text to make sure.

LITERAL COMPREHENSION

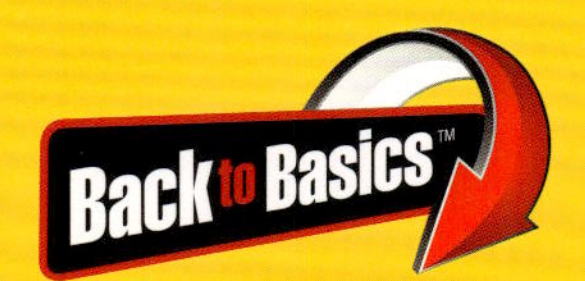

HIGH-FREQUENCY WORDS

YEAR 2

HIGH-FREQUENCY WORDS

YEAR 2

HIGH-FREQUENCY WORDS

YEAR 2

HIGH-FREQUENCY WORDS

YEAR 2

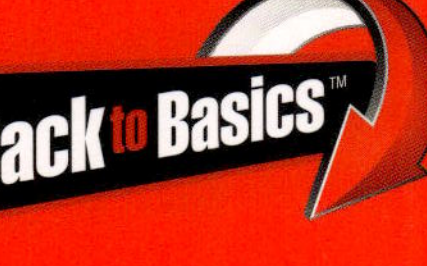

HIGH-FREQUENCY WORDS

YEAR 2

HIGH-FREQUENCY WORDS

YEAR 2

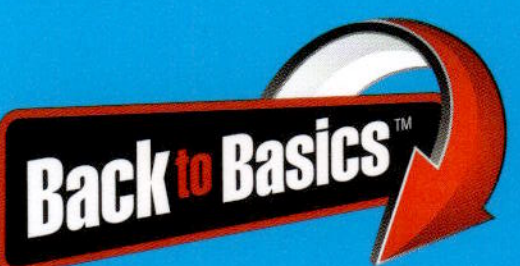

HIGH-FREQUENCY WORDS

YEAR 2

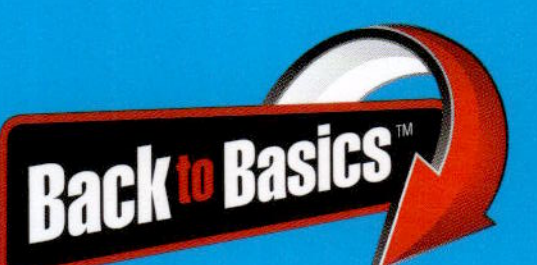

HIGH-FREQUENCY WORDS

YEAR 2

HIGH-FREQUENCY WORDS

YEAR 2

HIGH-FREQUENCY WORDS

YEAR 2

1 the
2 he
3 be
4 but
5 which

11 of
12 for
13 this
14 what
15 their

21 and
22 was
23 from
24 all
25 said

31 a
32 on
33 I
34 were
35 if

41 to
42 are
43 have
44 when
45 do

6 out
7 into
8 no
9 made
10 long

16 them
17 has
18 make
19 over
20 little

26 then
27 more
28 than
29 did
30 very

36 she
37 her
38 first
39 down
40 after

46 many
47 two
48 been
49 only
50 words

51 in
52 as
53 or
54 we
55 will

61 is
62 with
63 by
64 there
65 each

71 you
72 here
73 one
74 can
75 about

81 that
82 they
83 had
84 an
85 how

91 it
92 at
93 not
94 your
95 up

56 some
57 like
58 its
59 way
60 called

66 so
67 him
68 who
69 find
70 just

76 these
77 see
78 now
79 use
80 where

86 would
87 time
88 people
89 may
90 most

96 other
97 could
98 my
99 water
100 know

HIGH-FREQUENCY WORDS

YEAR 2

HIGH-FREQUENCY WORDS

YEAR 2

HIGH-FREQUENCY WORDS

YEAR 2

HIGH-FREQUENCY WORDS

YEAR 2

HIGH-FREQUENCY WORDS

YEAR 2

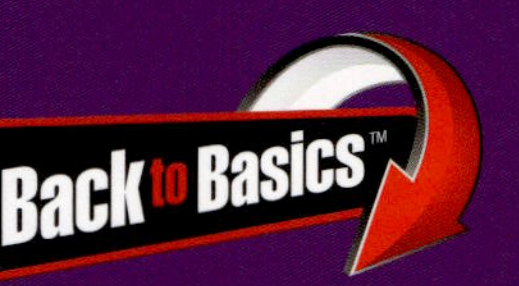
HIGH-FREQUENCY WORDS

YEAR 2

HIGH-FREQUENCY WORDS

YEAR 2

HIGH-FREQUENCY WORDS

YEAR 2

HIGH-FREQUENCY WORDS

YEAR 2

HIGH-FREQUENCY WORDS

YEAR 2

INTERPRETIVE COMPREHENSION

We understand what the text says and then link information or ideas together to get a greater meaning. We can then answer some more questions about the text.

Why would people be scared of earwigs?

People may have heard that earwigs crawl into your ear and eat your brain.

We can interpret this because the text tells us *They do not crawl into your ear and through to your brain to eat your brain while you are asleep!*

Why are earwigs an important part of the food chain?

Many creatures eat earwigs as a food source, so without them those creatures may die.

We can interpret this because the text tells us *Many animals eat earwigs – frogs, lizards, spiders, praying mantises, ants and some birds feed on earwigs regularly. They are an important part of the food chain.*

Do you agree with the interpretations and the answers? Check the text to make sure.

We can go back at any time to confirm what we understand.

APPLIED COMPREHENSION

We understand the text, then add what we have learned to what we already know and draw conclusions. We will be able to answer questions that go **beyond** the text.

Should people be afraid of earwigs?

No, people should not be afraid of earwigs because they are harmless.

The text tells us that *they are harmless to humans* and it also tells us what earwigs like to feed on. As people are not on this list, we can say that they are not a threat to people. We also know that they are small and we are big, so we could overcome them at any time.

Can you use what you already know to provide your own answers?

TRANSPORT

Read this with a grown-up and discuss any tricky words.

NON-FICTION

Vehicles, such as cars, buses, trains, planes and boats, transport us from one place to another.

Some people use transport to make short daily trips to work or school. Others use it for longer journeys, such as a holiday or a business trip overseas.

Public transport is designed for moving large groups of people. Buses, trains, trams, ferries and planes are types of public transport. Private transport includes cars, motorcycles and bicycles.

Did you know?
People who travel a long distance to and from work are known as **commuters**.

Did you know?
Many students use buses and trains to get to and from school.

Did you know?
The first living creatures to fly in a hot-air balloon were a sheep, a duck and a rooster.

GLOSSARY

vehicles	machines to move people
transport (verb)	carry someone or something from one place to another
daily	every day
journey	trip
overseas	another country
ferries	large boats that can carry people and cars over water
commuter	person who travels a long way to and from work every day

You practise

TOP TIP 6
Monitor your reading to make sure you understand.

What types of vehicles take us from one place to another?

Some of these vehicles are ______________________________

What is public transport designed for?

____

What are the types of public transport?

____

What are the types of private transport?

____

What is transport useful for?

____

Why is public transport important?

____

Why is private transport important?

____

Why were animals used to fly in the first hot-air balloons?

____

Would we be able to move without transport?

____

Why is it important to have transport?

____

BOB time!

VOCABULARY 3

HIGH-FREQUENCY WORDS 41–60

The words featured in this unit are on the yellow word cards.

Missing letters

Fill in the missing letters in the word bank words below.

to	do	only	or	like
are	many	words	we	its
have	two	in	will	way
when	been	as	some	called

a _ an _

b h _ v _

c b _ _ n

d _ al _ ed

e li _ _

f w _ en

g _ om _

h o _ ly

i _ _ rds

j t _ o

Word frames

Draw frames around each letter of these words to help you remember their shapes.

t o   a r e   h a v e   w h e n   d o

m a n y   t w o   b e e n   o n l y

w o r d s   i n   a s   o r   w e

c a l l e d   i t s   w a y   w i l l

s o m e   l i k e

BOB time!

QUICK QUIZ 3

Unit 9 **Pirate School** Unit 10 **Transport**

1 Word meanings

Match each word to its meaning by drawing a line between them.

a	pirate	weapon
b	surprises	workers on a boat
c	sword	shooting device
d	cannon	a robber who sails on a ship
e	crew	something unexpected

2 Fill the gaps

Read the sentences and then fill in the gaps with a word from the word bank.

cars buses trains planes boats

a ______________ are the most common type of transport.

b The harbour is crowded with ______________ on New Year's Eve.

c Our school hired two ______________ to take us on an excursion.

d I went to the airport to watch the ______________ take off and land.

e Old-fashioned steam ______________ are not used very much today.

BOB time!

REPTILES

Read this with a grown-up and discuss any tricky words.

NON-FICTION

Reptiles are cold-blooded animals with a backbone and scales.

All reptiles are cold-blooded animals. This means they need heat from outside their bodies. They use heat from the sun to warm their bodies.

All reptiles have scales to protect their bodies. The scales make a thick, tough skin. Reptiles live in warm or hot places. Some reptiles live in the desert. Some reptiles live in the sea.

Most reptiles lay eggs. The eggs have leathery shells. Reptiles lay their eggs on land. The shells protect the baby reptiles while they grow.

Did you know?
The smallest reptile is a British Island gecko. It is 1.7 centimetres long.

Did you know?
There are 6560 different species of reptile.

Did you know?
The basilisk lizard can run on water to escape its predators.

GLOSSARY

cold-blooded	needing to get heat from the sun
scales	thin, hard plates that cover the bodies of reptiles and fish
protect	save from danger
leathery	tough, like animal skin
gecko	type of lizard

You practise

TOP TIP 7
What is the purpose of the text?

1. What are three important features of reptiles?

Three features are that they ____________________

2. Where do reptiles get their body heat from?

____

3. Where do reptiles live?

____

4. What are reptile eggs like?

____

5. Do reptiles have protection for their bodies?

____

6. Do reptiles have protection for their babies?

____

7. Why do reptiles like to live in hot places?

____

8. What would a basilisk lizard do if it saw a crocodile coming?

____

9. Would reptiles be able to live in the snow?

____

10. What would you need to keep a reptile as a pet?

____

BOB time!

CHIMPANZEES

Read this with a grown-up and discuss any tricky words.

NON-FICTION

The mammal that is most like humans is the chimpanzee.

Like humans, chimpanzees use tools. They use sticks to pick termites and other insects out of their nests. They use stones to crack open nuts and fruits. Chimpanzees show emotions like humans. They can be kind, but they can also be aggressive and violent.

Chimpanzees live in groups. They spend a lot of time grooming each other. This removes parasites but also helps them to feel close, like a family.

Did you know?
Chimpanzees usually run on all fours but can walk upright as well.

Did you know?
Chimpanzees eat mostly fruit, termites and leaves but will also eat meat, including small animals they hunt and kill.

Did you know?
Chimpanzees use branches and leaves to build new sleeping nests each night.

Did you know?
A grown male chimpanzee can eat 50 bananas in one meal.

GLOSSARY

mammal	an animal, including humans, that has warm blood; young feed on mother's milk
termites	insects that feed on wood
aggressive	likely to attack
violent	using rough force
grooming	cleaning and taking care of appearance (look)
parasites	animals that live and feed on other animals
upright	standing up on two legs

You practise

TOP TIP 8
Decide if what you've read is fact or opinion.

What tools do chimpanzees use?

Chimpanzees use

Can chimpanzees show emotion?

Do chimpanzees live alone or in groups?

What do chimpanzees like to do that makes them feel like a family?

What are some ways that chimpanzees act like humans?

In what ways do chimpanzees look like humans?

Why would chimpanzees build a new sleeping nest each night?

Why do chimpanzees run on all fours instead of running upright?

Are we so interested in chimpanzees because they are like us?

Why would chimpanzees live in groups rather than alone?

BOB time!

UNIT 15

VOCABULARY 4

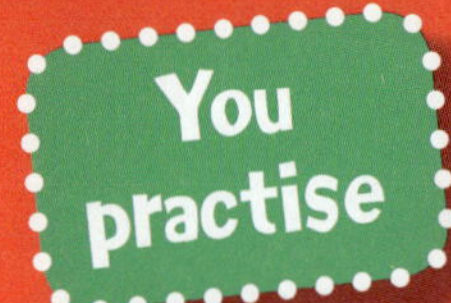

HIGH-FREQUENCY WORDS 61–80

The words featured in this unit are on the green word cards.

1 Alphabetical order

Write the words from the word bank in alphabetical order.

is	by	each	him	find
with	there	so	who	just

a by

b ______

c ______

d ______

e ______

f ______

g ______

h ______

i ______

j ______

2 Vowels and consonants

Write all the words from the word bank using a red pencil for the vowels (a, e, i, o, u) and a blue pencil for the consonants (all other letters).

you	one	about	see	use
here	can	these	now	where

you ______ ______ ______

______ ______ ______ ______

______ ______

BOB time!

You practise

QUICK QUIZ 4

Unit 13 Reptiles Unit 14 Chimpanzees

1 Word pictures

Create a snake by adding these words behind the snake's head.

reptiles backbone scales protect tough

Create a trail of ants by adding these words behind the ant.

sticks tools termites insects nests

2 Going backwards

Write these backwards words the right way and use each word in a sentence.

a niks ____________ ______________________________

b ylimaf ____________ ______________________________

c sgge ____________ ______________________________

d sevael ____________ ______________________________

e tneloiv ____________ ______________________________

f aes ____________ ______________________________

g dnik ____________ ______________________________

h sllehs ____________ ______________________________

i tiurf ____________ ______________________________

j tresed ____________ ______________________________

BOB time!

SURVIVING THE COLD

Read this with a grown-up and discuss any tricky words.

NON-FICTION

Some animals survive the winter on a mountain by hibernating. This means they sleep through the coldest months, living on the food they have stored.

Black bears in the mountains of North America hibernate every winter.

The bear eats as much as possible in summer and autumn.

In winter, when there is not much food left, the bear goes into a den to sleep. The den might be a cave, a burrow or the space under some logs on the ground.

The bear's breathing rate drops. It can be as slow as one breath every 45 seconds. It sleeps from four to seven months.

The bear comes out of the den in spring.

GLOSSARY

survive	not die
hibernating	sleeping for the whole winter
stored	put away
den	hidden home of a wild animal
breathing rate	the number of breaths in a certain time

You practise

TOP TIP 9
Create visual images of what you read

UNIT 17

1 How do some animals survive the winter?

Some animals survive the winter by ______________________

2 How often do the black bears of North America hibernate?

____

3 When do the black bears eat as much as possible?

____

4 Where might bears make their dens?

____

5 Why does the black bear hibernate?

____

6 Why would the black bear slow down its breathing?

____

7 Why does the black bear come out in spring?

____

8 What would a black bear want most when it came out of its den?

____

9 Is the black bear a clever animal?

____

10 What other animal do you know that lives on cold mountains?

____

BOB time!

ARCHITECTURE

Read this with a grown-up and discuss any tricky words.

NON-FICTION

Architecture is the art and science of designing buildings.

Many famous buildings become icons. The Sydney Opera House has become an icon of Australia.

In 1955 the state government decided that Sydney needed an opera house. It wanted one of the world's great buildings, so it ran a competition.

There were 233 design entries from 32 countries.

The winner was Jørn Utzon, a Danish architect. Work began in March 1959 at Bennelong Point on Sydney Harbour.

After a while, Utzon and the government began to disagree. Utzon resigned in 1966 and left Australia. The Sydney Opera House was meant to be finished by 1963, but it did not open until 1973.

More than four million people visit the Sydney Opera House each year.

In 2007, the building was named a UNESCO World Heritage site. This means that the Sydney Opera House is a building of outstanding importance.

Did you know?

The idea for the Opera House's shape came from a cut orange.

Did you know?

The Sydney Opera House has a concert hall, an opera theatre, three small theatres, shops and restaurants.

Did you know?

The white roof tiles were chosen to reflect the colours of the harbour.

GLOSSARY

architecture	the art and science of designing buildings
icon	a famous thing recognised all over the world
competition	a contest people take part in to try to win
design entries	the plan of the building entered into the competition
Danish	from the country of Denmark
resigned	left a job

You practise

TOP TIP 10
Summarise the most important ideas.

1. What is architecture?

   Architecture is the

2. What is one of the best known icons of Australia?

3. How did the government choose a design for the Opera House?

4. Who was the architect of the Sydney Opera House?

5. Was Utzon happy with the government's decisions about the Opera House?

6. Was the Sydney Opera House built on time?

7. How do we know this building is special?

8. Is the Sydney Opera House a tourist destination?

9. When people think of Sydney, what images would they think of?

10. Why is the Sydney Opera House so special?

BOB time!

VOCABULARY 5

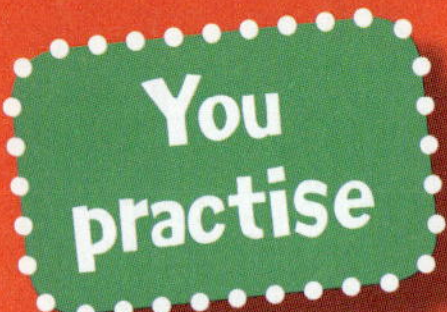

HIGH-FREQUENCY WORDS 81–100

The words featured in this unit are on the purple word cards.

1 Word frames

Find a word from the word bank to fit each word frame and write the letters in the boxes.

that	had	how	time	may
they	an	would	people	most

a 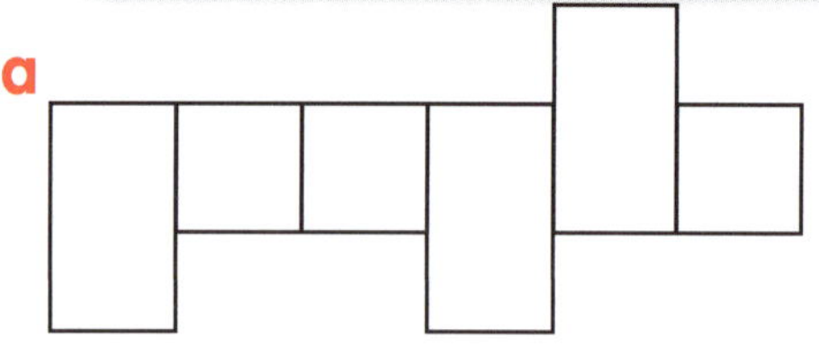

b 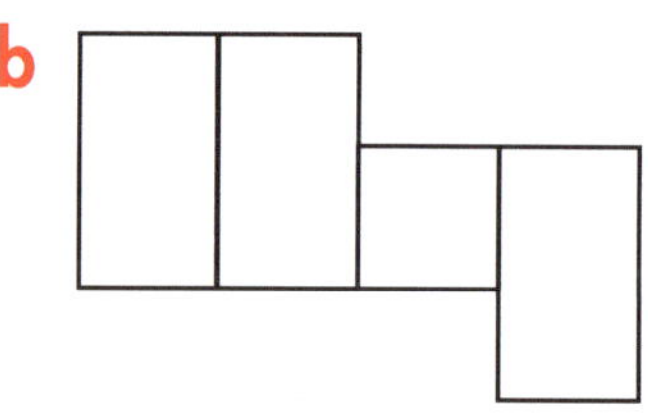

c 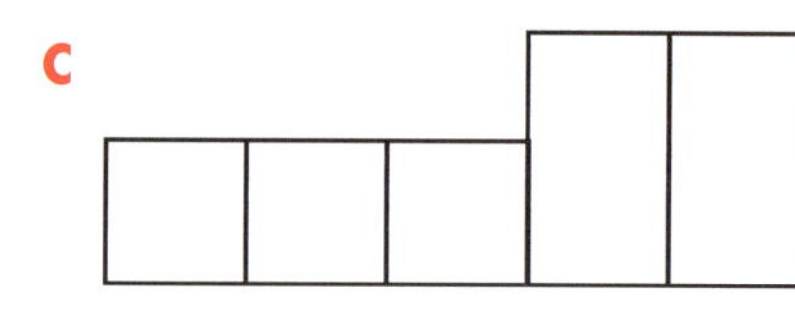

d 

e 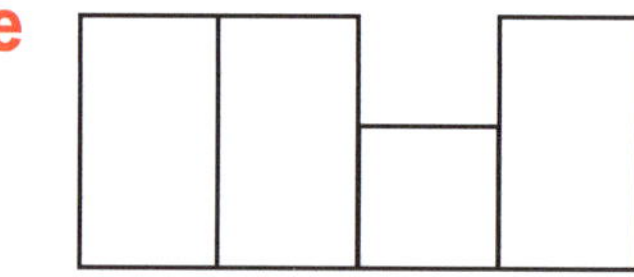

2 Spelling bees

Count the number of stripes on the bees and see which of these words have the same number of letters. Write the words in the spaces.

it at not your up other could my water know

BOB time!

QUICK QUIZ 5

Unit 17 **Surviving the Cold** Unit 18 **Architecture**

1 Interesting sentences

Write five sentences, each including two words from the word bank.

winter	animals	sleep	food	black
bears	den	cave	burrow	spring

a ______________________________

b ______________________________

c ______________________________

d ______________________________

e ______________________________

Syllables

Words are made up of sound "chunks", or syllables. Rewrite the words below showing their syllables, and note the number of syllables.

Word	Syllables	No.	Word	Syllables	No.
a buildings	build/ings	2	f harbour		
b winner			g visit		
c Opera			h icon		
d House			i Sydney		
e concert			j orange		

BOB time!

TEST 1

FICTION: RESTRUCTURING THE TEXT

★ Turn back to Unit 9 on page 22 and re-read Pirate School.
★ The text below is out of sequence. Put the paragraphs back in order by writing the paragraph numbers in the correct order in the boxes below.

☐ ☐ ☐ ☐ ☐ ☐

Pirate School

1 The crew all cheered as they sailed away.

2 Treasure-hunting class was on Friday. The crew were all happy to go to this class. Captain Red Beard was not very good at adding or subtracting. His sharing skills were also very bad. His teacher almost walked the plank!

3 First was sword-fighting class. Captain Red Beard cut his finger. He did not like the sight of blood. His legs went wobbly. His crew got wobbly legs too. Barnacle Bill shook his head and raised his sword. "What kind of pirates are you?" he cried.

4 When Barnacle Bill came aboard, the crew of *The Black Beast* got a huge surprise. Barnacle Bill was the head of the Pirate School ship and he wasn't happy. "Whirling whales!" said Barnacle Bill. "What kind of pirates are you? You have forgotten how to be bold, fierce and nasty pirates. It's back to school for the lot of you."

5 That night, Captain Red Beard and his crew remembered how to be pirates. They showed Barnacle Bill exactly what kind of pirates they were. Quickly and quietly, they set to work stealing Barnacle Bill's treasure. "Thanks for the treasure!" shouted Captain Red Beard. "You see we are bold, fierce and clever pirates!"

6 Then there was a cannon-firing class. The Captain's red beard got burnt when the cannon fired. Black soot covered the crew. "Now you're looking like a crew of fierce pirates!" said Colin the cannon master. Barnacle Bill just shook his head. "What kind of pirates are you?" he cried.

BOB time!

TEST 2

NON-FICTION: RESTRUCTURING THE TEXT

★ Turn back to Unit 17 on page 36 and re-read Surviving the Cold.
★ The following text is out of sequence. Put the paragraphs back in order by writing the paragraph numbers in the correct order in the boxes below.

Surviving the Cold

1 In winter, when there is not much food left, the bear goes into a den to sleep. The den might be a cave, a burrow or the space under some logs on the ground.

2 The bear comes out of the den in spring.

3 Some animals survive the winter on a mountain by hibernating. This means they sleep through the coldest months, living on the food they have stored.

4 The bear eats as much as possible in summer and autumn.

5 The bear's breathing rate drops. It can be as slow as one breath every 45 seconds. It sleeps from four to seven months.

6 Black bears in the mountains of North America hibernate every winter.

BOB time!

HIGH-FREQUENCY WORDS

Ask an adult to read you the high-frequency words in blocks of 20 and write each word in its correct box. Start with the red cards (words 1–20), then the blue cards (words 21–40), the yellow cards (words 41–60), the green cards (words 61–80) and finally the purple cards (words 81–100).

1	21	41	61	81
2	22	42	62	82
3	23	43	63	83
4	24	44	64	84
5	25	45	65	85
6	26	46	66	86
7	27	47	67	87
8	28	48	68	88
9	29	49	69	89
10	30	50	70	90
11	31	51	71	91
12	32	52	72	92
13	33	53	73	93
14	34	54	74	94
15	35	55	75	95
16	36	56	76	96
17	37	57	77	97
18	38	58	78	98
19	39	59	79	99
20	40	60	80	100

ANSWERS

Unit 1 – The Great Balancing Act

1. The monkeys belonged to Wonderful Wilma.
2. Edna was an elephant.
3. The wind made the flagpole sway.
4. Max Manyhands used his juggling chairs and a hoop to try to reach the monkeys.
5. The monkeys would not let go of the flagpole because they were too frightened.
6. Edna swooshed at the fly with her trunk because it was annoying her.
7. Bendy Betty is probably very flexible (able to bend) for her circus act.
8. The monkeys happily went to Grandpa Zoomelli because he was at just the right height.
9. Yes the monkeys were in danger because they were up a flagpole and it was very windy.
10. Answers may vary. Yes, all the circus performers risked their lives trying to save the monkeys, because they were balancing high up and it was windy.

Unit 2 – Crazy Chewing Gum

1. Declan found the recipe on the internet.
2. Declan yelled at Blackie for sticking her nose in the drawer, ruining the chewing gum mixture.
3. Blackie's nose got bright pink chewing gum stuck all over it.
4. Declan's father's suit got chewing gum from Blackie's paw stuck on it.
5. Declan's mother was cross because he wasn't supposed to do experiments and the chewing gum glue was getting on everything.
6. Declan's father was cross because the chewing gum glue had ruined his new suit.
7. The dentist was cross because his drill overheated trying to get Declan's teeth apart.
8. The chewing gum was stickier than usual because the powder mixed with it and made it like glue.
9. Answers may vary. Yes, the mess was Blackie's fault because she caused the sticky mixture and got it all over her nose. OR No, the mess was Declan's fault because he was the one making the chewing gum.
10. Answers may vary. If Declan experiments with carpet cleaner, something will probably go wrong and he'll upset his family again.

Unit 3 – Vocabulary 1

Answers will vary.

Unit 4 – Quick Quiz 1

2. a) chewing b) gum c) smell d) drill e) jumps f) pink g) glue h) nose i) dentist j) computer

Unit 5 – The Gwibber

1. Gog was excited because he had found a Gwibber in the forest.
2. Binks was worried that the Gwibber would eat them out of house and home, eating everything!
3. Binks didn't think Gog needed a guard dog because he is a giant.
4. The Gwibber ate all the beans in the vegetable patch when he flew off the roof.
5. The water in the pond was important to Binks as the fish would die without it.
6. Binks was upset because the Gwibber dug a big hole to sleep in and ruined the garden.
7. The Gwibber wanted to go inside and find Gog and Binks to keep him company.
8. Answers may vary. No, Gog would not miss the Gwibber because he was too much trouble. OR Yes, Gog would miss the Gwibber because it was exciting having a new creature as a pet.
9. Binks said "Muddy pups!" as an elf exclamation, like we might say "Oh my gosh!".
10. Binks could relax and sleep well because all the excitement had died down and the Gwibber was no longer screeching and howling all night.

Unit 6 – The Big Kidnap

1. Pebble wouldn't go to bed because she was too busy having fun being wild in the jungle.
2. When Luna tried to get Pebble to go to bed she just laughed wildly and got louder.
3. The plan was that the dinosaurs would trap Pebble in a net and carry her to the top of a hill, then Tickles would fly her over the mountain to the other side of the island and put her on a soft bed of feathers, where Luna would sing to her and Leo would give her hot milk.
4. When Pebble was trapped in the net she screeched at them to let her go.
5. Yes, Pebble was happy in the jungle because she swung and laughed and didn't want to go to bed.
6. Yes, the dinosaurs looked after Pebble by putting her on a soft bed of feathers, giving her hot milk and singing her to sleep.
7. Luna was singing a lullaby to try to put Pebble to sleep.
8. All the dinosaurs fell asleep too because it was nice and quiet and they were so tired from chasing Pebble around.
9. Answers may vary. Yes, Pebble was naughty because she would not go to bed when asked to and did not think of others and stopped them sleeping. OR No, Pebble was not naughty, she was just having fun.
10. Answers may vary. Yes, the plan was too mean as it would be scary to be trapped in a net and flown over a mountain. OR No, the plan was not too mean as the dinosaurs were gentle with her and they got her to go to sleep.

Unit 7 – Vocabulary 2

1. a) her b) down c) all d) then e) more f) after g) she h) first i) from j) on

ANSWERS

Unit 8 – Quick Quiz 2

1.

e	x	c	i	t	e	d	r	s	s	e
h	s	q	u	i	c	k	l	y	h	a
u	w	p	s	r	f	o	r	e	s	t
h	o	u	s	e	s	k	t	l	e	g
t	u	p	n	d	h	h	o	l	e	s
f	i	s	h	g	e	l	r	e	d	i
n	t	a	c	t	i	e	e	d	l	c

2. plan; wild; jungle; island; sleep; songs; louder; feathers; yelled; net

Unit 9 – The Pirate School

1. Barnacle Bill was head of the Pirate School ship.
2. Barnacle Bill thought the crew had forgotten how to be bold, fierce and nasty pirates.
3. Barnacle Bill sent them all to attend classes at the Pirate School.
4. The crew of *The Black Beast* attended sword-fighting class, cannon-firing class and treasure-hunting class.
5. No, Captain Red Beard was not good at fighting because when he cut his finger his legs went wobbly because he did not like the sight of blood.
6. Yes, Barnacle Bill wanted the pirates to be bold, fierce and nasty.
7. Answers may vary. Yes, the pirates were smart because they tricked Barnacle Bill and stole the treasure. OR No, the pirates were not smart because they couldn't sword fight or fire the cannon or hunt for treasure very well.
8. The crew of *The Black Beast* would have been laughing at Barnacle Bill because they stole his treasure and sailed away.
9. Answers may vary. Yes, the classes did make the pirates bold, fierce and nasty because they stole the treasure and sailed away. OR No, the classes did not make the pirates bold, fierce and nasty because they quietly stole the treasure and sailed away at night, instead of fighting Barnacle Bill for it.
10. Answers may vary. Yes, Barnacle Bill would follow *The Black Beast* to get his treasure back. OR No, Barnacle Bill would not follow the pirates because he knew he had lost the treasure forever.

Unit 10 – Transport

1. Some vehicles that take us from one place to another are cars, buses, trains, planes and boats.
2. Public transport is designed for moving large groups of people.
3. Types of public transport include buses, trains, trams, ferries and planes.
4. Types of private transport include cars, motorcycles and bicycles.
5. Transport is useful for moving people or things from one place to another as quickly and easily as possible.
6. Answers may vary. Public transport allows large groups of people to travel over short or long distances at a reasonable cost and keeps traffic and pollution to a minimum.
7. Answers may vary. Private transport allows people to move around when and how they choose. In some places public transport is not available.
8. Animals were used so that human life was not in danger should the balloon fail.
9. Yes, we would be able to move without transport but only by walking or running, so only over short distances and taking a lot more time.
10. Answers may vary. Transport is important so that we can travel to work or school, so goods such as food can be taken to remote places and traded overseas, and so we can visit faraway places.

Unit 11 – Vocabulary 3

1. a) many b) have c) been d) called e) like f) when g) some h) only i) words j) two

Unit 12 – Quick Quiz 3

1. a) pirate – a robber who sails on a ship
   b) surprises – something unexpected
   c) sword – weapon
   d) cannon – shooting device
   e) crew – workers on a boat
2. a) cars b) boats c) buses d) planes e) trains

Unit 13 – Reptiles

1. Three features of reptiles are that they are cold-blooded, they have scales covering their bodies and most lay eggs.
2. Reptiles get their body heat from the sun.
3. Reptiles live in warm or hot places.
4. Reptile eggs have leathery shells.
5. Yes, reptiles have scales, which are like a tough, thick skin, to protect their bodies.
6. Yes, reptile eggs have tough, leathery shells that protect the babies while they grow.
7. Reptiles like to live in hot places so they can keep their bodies warm.
8. To escape from the crocodile the basilisk lizard could run away on the water.
9. No, reptiles would not be able to live in the snow as they couldn't get enough heat from their surroundings to warm their body.
10. To keep a reptile as a pet you would need a safe, warm or hot place to keep it and the right food to feed it.

Unit 14 – Chimpanzees

1. Chimpanzees use tools such as sticks to pick up termites and other insects from their nests, and stones to crack open nuts and fruits.
2. Yes, chimpanzees can be kind but they can also be aggressive and violent.
3. Chimpanzees live in groups like families.
4. Chimpanzees spend a lot of time grooming each other, which makes them feel close, like a family.
5. Answers may vary. Chimpanzees act like humans because they use tools, such as sticks and stones; they show emotions; they live in groups and groom one another; they can walk upright; they eat fruit and meat; they sometimes hunt and kill animals to eat.

ANSWERS

6. Answers may vary. Chimpanzees have similar hands, feet, face, ears, mouth, tongue, nose, eyes and facial expressions to humans.
7. Answers may vary. Chimpanzees build a new nest every night so they have a fresh place to sleep, which is more comfortable and clean; they also may enjoy the task of building.
8. Chimpanzees would run on all fours because it would be faster than trying to run standing upright.
9. Answers may vary. Yes, it is interesting to compare such similar behaviour in animals and humans, and to find out how intelligent chimpanzees are.
10. Answers may vary. Chimpanzees live in groups for protection; because they are social animals; for fun; to share the jobs; to help one another; to be happy.

Unit 15 – Vocabulary 4

1. a) by b) each c) find d) him e) is f) just g) so h) there i) who j) with
2. you, here, one, can, about, these, see, now, use, where

Unit 16 – Quick Quiz 4

2. a) skin b) family c) eggs d) leaves e) violent f) sea g) kind h) shells i) fruit j) desert

Unit 17 – Surviving the Cold

1. Some animals survive the winter by hibernating.
2. Black bears hibernate every year in winter from four to seven months.
3. Black bears eat as much food as possible in summer and autumn.
4. Black bears might make their dens in caves, burrows or spaces under logs on the ground.
5. Black bears hibernate because the winter is too cold and there isn't enough food.
6. Black bears slow down their breathing so they use less energy and keep warmer.
7. Black bears come out of hibernation in spring because the snow starts melting, it is warmer and there is more food to be found.
8. The thing a bear would want most would be food!
9. Answers may vary. Yes, black bears are very clever to sleep through the cold winter conditions, to store their food so they do not starve and to slow their breathing rate to save energy.
10. Answers may vary. Other animals that live in cold mountain areas include moose, elk, deer, oxen, goats, sheep, foxes and rabbits.

Unit 18 – Architecture

1. Architecture is the art and science of designing buildings.
2. The Sydney Opera House is one of the best known icons of Australia.
3. The government chose the design for the new opera house by running a competition.
4. Jørn Utzon, a Danish architect, was the architect of the Sydney Opera House.
5. No, Utzon and the government disagreed about how the Sydney Opera House should be built.
6. No, the opening of the Sydney Opera House was delayed by ten years.
7. We know the Sydney Opera House is important because it has been named a UNESCO World Heritage site.
8. Yes, the Sydney Opera House is a very popular tourist destination, with more than four million visitors each year.
9. Answers may vary. When people think of Sydney, Australia, they would think of the Sydney Opera House, as well as the Sydney Harbour Bridge and the 2000 Olympic Games.
10. Answers may vary. The Sydney Opera House is such a special building because it is very unusual and spectacular looking, it is on the beautiful Sydney Harbour, its white tiles can be lit up at night, and many special events are held there.

Unit 19 – Vocabulary 5

1. a) people b) they c) would d) an e) that
2. Two stripes: it, at, up, my. Three stripes: not. Four stripes: your, know. Five stripes: other, could, water.

Unit 20 – Quick Quiz 5

2. a) build / ings (2)
   b) win / ner (2)
   c) op / er / a (3)
   d) house (1)
   e) con / cert (2)
   f) har / bour (2)
   g) vis / it (2)
   h) i / con (2)
   i) Syd / ney (2)
   j) o / range (2)

Test 1 Comprehension

4, 3, 6, 2, 5, 1

Test 2 Comprehension

3, 6, 4, 1, 5, 2

Test 3 High-Frequency Words

Use the numbered high-frequency word cards to check the correct answers.